At The Going Down of the Sun

GW00801658

Becky Bishop

At the Going Down of the Sun

A collection of war poems

At the Going Down of the Sun

At the Going Down of the Sun

Dedication

Dedicated to the families and friends left
behind when the men and women went to
war and in memory of all their lost loved
ones.

At the Going Down of the Sun

At the Going Down of the Sun

Introduction

"They shall grow not old, as we that are left grow old:
Age shall not weary them, nor the years condemn.
At the going down of the sun and in the morning
We will remember them"
(from For the Fallen by Robert Laurence Binyon)

This well-known stanza, the inspiration behind the title of this book, has long been associated with the two World Wars and remembrance, the poem from which it is from having been written in 1914 in honour of the casualties of the Battle of Mons and Battle of the Marne. Since then this particular stanza has been used as a tribute for all casualties of war.

Inspired by this poem and my own war poet relatives, such as Julian Grenfell and Ivar Campbell, I have written a selection of poems about World War One and Two, some of which are dedicated to specific relatives.

I hope you enjoy reading them and seeing the photographs from a recent battlefield tour to France and Belgium.

At the Going Down of the Sun

Contents

Daddy's Girls
In memory of Private Ernest Piggott

We're watching at the window, we're waiting
by the door,
For you to come home, from the mighty war.

Waiting to see your shadow, walking up the
path,
For all the fun we'll have, you always make us
laugh.

We know you're fighting for the country, you
have a job to do,
Fighting for a better future, for us, your
precious two.

When you have to go back after leave, we hate
to see you go,
For when you're away, oh how we miss you
so.

But you haven't come home today, Mummy's
upset and sad,
You've been reported missing, killed by
someone bad.

Our lives once full of childish fun, have in a
moment, been torn apart,
And now and in the future, you'll just be a
memory in our hearts.

You won't be able to read to us at bedtime, or
help soothe us to sleep,
Or wipe away our tears, when of you, we
mourn and weep.

You won't be able to help with schoolwork, or
go through our teenage years,
Encourage all our dreams, and alleviate our
fears.

You won't see us get married, or have a
family of our own,
For we'll always be your little girls, you won't
see us fully grown.

And when we're feeling down, a prayer to
you, we'll say aloud,
For Daddy, we'll never forget you, you've
made your two little girls so proud.

2ᴺᴰ LIEUT. D. R. LEATHERDALE
1ˢᵗ R. W. KENT
MISSING SINCE JULY 22, 1916.

The Somme – 100 Years On

In memory of Donald and Alan Leatherdale

100 years ago, a deadly battle did commence,
Our soldiers were called to arms and went out
on the defence.

Skies were darkened and the ground smeared
red,
As shots rang out and men fell down dead.

So many lives lost, in just the first day alone,
So many young men, who'd never return
home.

For months and months, the battle raged on,
Our soldiers fought bravely and remained
ever strong.

The death toll would be high, in the Battle of
The Somme,
In what would be known as, the bloodiest
battle of World War One.

Families torn apart, a nation mourning the cost,

100 years on, we remember all those lives lost.

We may look back with sadness and mourn at their graves,

But most of all we remember with pride, for they were the bravest of the brave.

Is there news of my Boy?

In memory of Pilot Officer Charles Grant
Leatherdale

Is there news of my boy? He's a fighter in the
skies,
He's been declared missing, I don't know if he
lives or dies.

Is there news of my boy? His plane crashed to
the ground,
Some bodies were recovered, but my boy's
hasn't yet been found.

Is there news of my boy? Many months have
now gone by,
I still hold out hope, I refuse to mourn and
cry.

Is there news of my boy? It's been over a year
since his plane was lost,
I'm still waiting for news, but nothing's come
in the post.

Is there news of my boy? The day has finally
come,
He's officially been declared dead and won't
be coming home.

Is there news of my boy? It's been five years
and I still hold out hope,
For without hope, I don't know how I'd cope

Is there news of my boy? I'll never give up on
him, you see,
For he was my brave, beloved boy and means
the world to me.

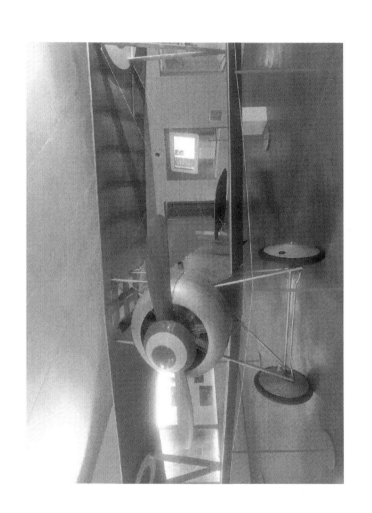

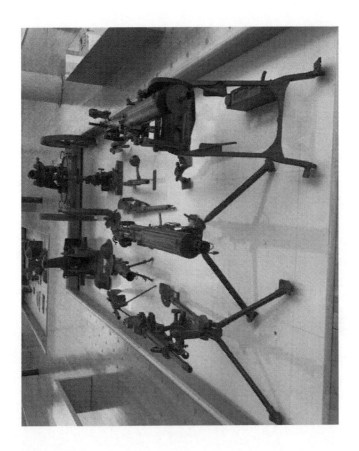

Was the war worth his life?

In memory of Private Herbert Edward

Pennyfather

Beneath a grassy bank, a soldier's body lies,

Alone and forgotten, nothing to mark where

he died.

As he lies on the ground, his dog tags washed

away by the mud and rain,

He's just another soldier, one without a name.

For he's one of the missing, those who are

presumed dead,

Killed in the midst of battle, a bullet to the

head.

And for his family, there's still a grain of
hope,
They pray he's alive, otherwise they don't
know how they'll cope.

They think back proudly, to the day he first
went on parade,
But as the months go by, the hope they once
had starts to fade.

Sometime down the line, they've received the
news they dread,
That their beloved boy, is officially declared
dead.

They weep with sorrow and anger, their boy
has paid the price,
And for what, they ask themselves, was the
war really worth his life.

Fighting for our country

In memory of Rifleman Thomas M Topping

We fought for our country, we did our very best,
And now we're in a cemetery, where we're laid to rest.

Row upon row, we lie side by side,
And come each November, we're remembered with pride.

Some aren't so lucky, they don't even get a grave,
Just a name on a memorial, that honours all the brave.

From different battalions, regiments and countries too,
United in battle, in death we are too.

The battles we fought, the ones we lost and won,
Are now a part of history, time has since moved on.

A generation lost, some of us still in our teens,
When we went to war and saw horrors we shouldn't have seen.

Families torn apart, their hearts full of grief,
As they mourn their loved one, whose life was oh so brief.

But although now we're just a memory, that's forever in the past,
We fought for a better future and left a legacy that'll last.

Ghosts of Soldiers Past

In memory of John Jasper and Charles Frederick Stocker

There's a stillness in the air, the landscape
calm and quiet,
A sense of peace, belying the horrors that
went on.

What was a field of bloodshed, is now a field
of grass,
And marching on the gentle breeze, the ghosts
of soldiers past.

Passing through where once they fought, but
now go unseen, unheard,
The land which claimed them years before,
now they're just a memory in our hearts.

Once it was a battleground, where comrades
were maimed and killed,
And now all that's left, are crater holes in the
ground

A poppy wreath lies on the ground, to
remember all those lost,
And somewhere in the distance, a bugler
plays the last post

Goodbye Dearest Mother
In memory of Private Cecil George Gollege

Goodbye dearest mother, the time has now
come,
For me to go off to fight, my journey has
begun.

Goodbye dearest mother, I'm marching on my
way,
And hope against hope, that I'll be home
some day.

Goodbye dearest mother, I'm wearing the
uniform you pressed,
The pride on your face, when you saw me
smartly dressed.

Goodbye dearest mother, from the trench I
write,
The fighting is relentless, with no end in sight.

Goodbye dearest mother, it's dark and lonely
here,
So many miles away, how I wish that you
were near.

Goodbye dearest mother, there's bombing
overhead,
So many of my comrades, wounded and left
for dead.

Goodbye dearest mother, I think today might
be my last,
And then I'll just be a memory, fading into the
past.

Goodbye dearest mother, if you no longer hear from me,

A telegram will be sent, and nineteen I'll forever be.

Goodbye dearest mother, forever we may be apart,

But always remember, I love you with all my heart.

Unknown Soldier

In memory of Private James Seed

I am an unknown soldier, one who couldn't
be saved,
Missing presumed killed, I have no plaque or
grave.

Just a name on a memorial, is all that's left to
see,
And aged twenty, is all I'll ever be.

Frozen in time, I'll never get to grow old,
But hopefully one day, my story can be told.

Telling of my life, so I'll be more than just an
unknown face,
And down in the history books, I'll forever
have a place.

Battle Worn

Battle worn and weary, in the trenches I lie,
As all round me, my comrades fall and die.

Mud and rain seep through my clothes and
chill me to the bone,
How I wish I was back, in the comfort of my
home.

But so much has happened, since the day I
left,
The memory of my family, makes me feel
quite bereft.

A Soldier's War

Soldiers of all ages, some not even out of their teens,

Were called up to fight, to face horrors yet unseen.

All suited and booted, marching off proudly they did go,

For those left behind, the worry and tears tried not to show.

Travelling across land and sea, meeting foe and friend,

Risking their lives, for their country they did defend.

Under the moonlit sky, against a rising sun,

Amidst the dust and dirt, battles raged on.

Gunfire and bombings, became the sounds of war,

All it took was one moment and lives were changed for evermore.

Skies grew darkened, the ground turning red,

Bullets whizzing overhead, soldiers falling
down dead.

Homesick and wounded, soldiers struggled to
survive,

So much bloodshed and so many not making
it out alive.

For friends and family, waiting anxiously at
home,

Fearing for news, that their loved one was
gone.

And for those that return, the life they once
knew, is no more,

From lost limbs to lost friends, all thanks to
the destruction called war.

So each year come November, we remember
with pride,

The brave and the mighty, who fought and
who died.

At the Going Down of the Sun

Under an Alias

In memory of Private Alick Hilton Leatherdale

Orphaned at nine, in the Navy at eighteen,
Then went AWOL, ran away from who I'd been.

Setting sail for Canada, leaving behind all the strife,
Under an alias, I begin my new life.

Two years later war breaks out, I join up to fight,
Fighting for my country, doing what's right.

Then I was killed in action and it was only after I'd died,
That officials found out, about my name I had lied!

In a Field of Poppies

In a field of poppies, there's one brighter than
all the rest,
It's in memory of a soldier, who was the very
best.

He signed up to fight, knowing he could lose
his life,
And one day amongst the battlefields, he
made his sacrifice.

For his family, their lives have been torn
apart,
His loss is hard to bear, there's now a hole in
their heart.

At the table, they still lay him a place,
And all that remains, is a picture of his face.

Staring out from the mantelpiece, frozen in
time, he remains forever young,
But always remembered, at the going down of
the sun.

A Girl from Meavy

In memory of Armorel Avice Kitty Treveylan

She was a girl from Meavy, Kitty was her name,
She was a girl from Meavy, whose life changed when war came.
She was a girl from Meavy, a pretty girl she'd been,
She was a girl from Meavy, who left home at seventeen.
She was a girl from Meavy, who went to France and worked in the canteens,
She was a girl from Meavy, who fell ill and died aged nineteen.

Following in his footsteps

In memory of Captain Neill Adrian
Mountstuart Grant-Duff

I was a boy, of just four years old,
When one day, sad news I was told.

The Daddy that I hardly knew,
Would never again, walk through the door.

As I grow up, Mum keeps his memory alive,
A part of our family, even though he didn't
survive.

And so the years past by, until finally I am,
The same age as my Dad, when war first
began.

Another war is now looming, I'll sign up and
enlist,
Fight like my Dad did, whatever the risk.

He may be long gone, but a part of him, in
me, will always remain,
I'll fight for my country, I won't let his death
be in vain.

We'll Meet Again

We'll meet again, one sunny day,
We'll meet again, in a land faraway,
We'll meet again, where skies are blue,
We'll meet again, where planes once flew.

In a park by a bench, two people take a seat,
Two people who thought, never again would
they meet.
At last reunited, one's aged, one's young,
One died of old age, the other was killed by a
gun.

One died on the battlefield, the other at home,
United in death, they both died alone.
The years may have past and kept them apart,
But they've always remained, in each other's
hearts.

The rest of their journey, they can walk now
as one,
A couple at last, reunited at the going down of
the sun.

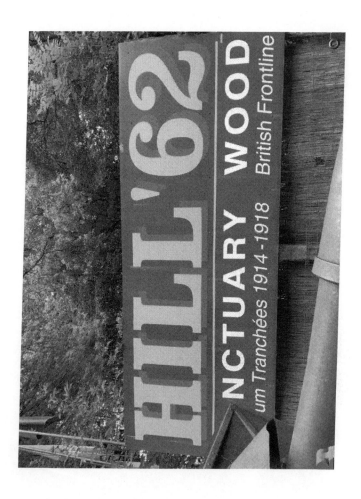

Last Letter Home

She stands at the window, tears running
down her cheeks,
The news she's been given, leaves her at a loss
to speak.

Pieces of paper in her hand, flutter to the
ground,
The news of his death, will have echoes far
around.

The pages are from a letter, the very last from
her son,
Before he was killed, by a German sniper gun.

Dear Mother, hope you're well, the letter began,
Give my love to Dad, Sissy and Gran.

I'm doing ok, don't worry about me,
But can you send some socks, biscuits and tea.

We're preparing to launch an attack, it'll be very
soon,
Going over the front, under the light of the moon.

We'll creep up on the enemy and hopefully kill the
swine,
Don't worry about me, I'm sure I'll be fine.

But in case I'm not, if I'm injured or die,
Don't mourn for long, don't sit and cry.

Just celebrate and remember me, for I've had a
great life,
Even if at times, I've caused you and Dad strife!

Know you were the best parents, I could have
asked for,
And as for Sissy, you know her I adore.

I knew what could happen, when I went to enlist,
But I wanted to do my bit, that's why I took the
risk.

So it's goodbye for now, I've got to be on my way,
I'll write again soon, if not, may we meet again one
day.

A little girl comes into the room, eyes wide
and sad,
She heard her mother's cries and knows the
news must be bad.

A family in mourning, their grief is all too
raw,
Of a beloved only son and brother, who sadly
is no more.

At the table, there'll always be an extra place,
His death will leave a void, no one can ever
replace.

As time passes by, as the family grows up and
grows old,
There's always a missing member, whose
story has to be told.

Of a young boy, whose life was taken too
soon,
They make a pilgrimage to his grave, each
year come June.

His photo and last letter home, take pride of
place in their front room,
A daily reminder, of the day their lives were
plunged into gloom.

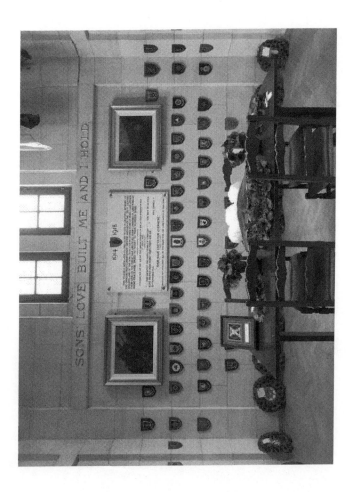

The Final Resting Place

A barren land, underneath a darkened sky,
Now the final resting place, of those who
died.

Where battles were fought and lives were lost,
In the war to end all wars, no matter what the
cost.

Now they lie side by side, row upon row,
Where all is quiet, except for a crow.

Of men and boys, some with no name,
Who in the battles, were killed and maimed.

Visitors come, to find a grave,
Of a family member, who couldn't be saved.

And when they're gone, all's quiet again,
A barren land, except when it rains.

It brings the flowers into bloom,
A splash of colour, amongst the gloom.

A sense of peace and calm; for them there is
no more war to fight.
The land looks after them and holds them
forever tight.

What could I have been if I hadn't gone to war?

I could have been a lawyer, fighting rights
and wrongs,
Or a star of the stage, singing great songs.

I could have been a fireman, putting out fires,
Instead I'm on the battlefield, cutting through
wires.

I could have been a typist, I was quicker than
all the rest,
Or a teacher, helping children to be their best.

I could have been a postman, delivering my
rounds,
But instead I'm just a body, buried in the
ground.

I could have been a fisherman, working in
different ports,
I could have been anything, had my life not
been cut short.

The Only One Left

In memory of all those who joined Pals Battalions

Babes in arms the five of us were, when we became friends,
And growing up, we knew we'd be friends until the end.

We played in each other's houses and outside in the street,
Kicking a football and eating lots of sweets.

And when war came, we didn't let it split us apart,
We joined the same battalion, united in playing our part.

Young and carefree, off to training we went,

And then to France and Belgium, we just went

where we were sent.

First there was Loos, where Frank lost his life,

Leaving behind, his new young wife.

Then there was the Somme, where Billy was

shot through the head,

And George was missing, before being

declared dead.

Billy was a joker, he liked to have fun,

And George was his parents', beloved only

son.

Next came Passchendaele, where Harry was

killed on the last day,

He left a young wife and a child on the way.

Now out of the five, I'm the only one who
remains,
The life we once knew, will never be the same.

It's 1918 now, I'm lucky to have survived this
long,
Never knowing if the next attack, could be my
swansong.

The months have gone by, the War's at an
end, I've survived,
But each day I remember, my mates who
didn't make it out alive.

Forever young they'll remain, whilst I get to
grow old,
Their sacrifice mustn't be forgotten, their
stories must always be told.

Frank's wife remarried and had three
strapping sons,
One was named Frank, a tribute to my pal
killed by a gun.

George's parents never recovered, they died
within a few years,
Reunited with their son, they no longer shed
tears.

Harry's wife remained true to him, until the
day she died,
And over the years, for him a thousand tears
she has cried.

His child, a son, grew up and fought in World
War Two,
Making his Dad proud, he won a medal or
two.

As I grow old and take my last breath,
My old pals will be waiting, to greet me in
death.

With open arms they'll welcome me, the five
of us together once more,
Reunited at last and for evermore.

Marching through the streets

In towns and villages throughout the country,
soldiers go marching through the streets,
Proudly wearing their uniforms, giving a
salute to those they meet.

Lining the streets are friends and family,
neighbours and shopkeepers too,
Giving their boys a send-off, some are losing a
son or two.

They wave them off to war, first to a training
camp,
Then to France and Belgium, where
conditions are muddy and damp.

As the war years go by, telegrams are
delivered to many doors,
Delivering bad news, to both the rich and
poor.

And then the day comes, when the war ends
at last,
The soldiers return home, except the ones lost
to the past.

They arrive back by train, their families they
greet,
To welcome them home, there's a party in the
street.

For those that returned, life goes on, though
not quite the same,
And each year in November, the lost ones
they remember by name.

Aguila Wren

In memory of Isabel Mary Milne-Home

Her name was Isabel, she had dark, wavy
hair,
A popular personality and a complexion fair.

She worked with girl guides, until the war
came,
When she joined the Wrens, a Third Officer
she became.

She helped train top Wrens to be
telegraphists, there were a select few,
They took part in a course, only the best made
it through.

One day in August, twenty-one Wrens waited
on the quay,
Boarded the ship Aguila and set sail on the
sea.

Bound for cypher duties in Gibraltar, when
they were attacked by a torpedo,
It struck the ship and tore it in two.

The ship sank within minutes, none of the
Wrens survived,
Third Officer Isabel, was just twenty-three
when she died.

A lifeboat was named after them, a tribute to
the Wrens who died,
A lasting legacy and reminder, for those that
survived.

Dig for Victory

In memory of all the Land Girls

Let's all dig for victory, we'll show Hitler how
it's done,
Let's all dig for victory, this war soon we'll
have won.

Let's all dig for victory, we'll toil and plant the
land,
Let's all dig for victory, we have to lend a
helping hand.

Let's all dig for victory, us women are just as
good,
Let's all dig for victory, for the country we'll
provide food.

Let's all dig for victory and when the war is done,

Let's all dig for victory, we'll show Hitler that we've won!

At the Going Down of the Sun

Acknowledgements

Beverley Hill

Clifford Jones

St Alban the Martyr Church

Sue Robinson

Nicola Waddington

Wenches in Trenches

At the Going Down of the Sun

Dear Reader

If you have enjoyed reading this book, then please leave a review on Amazon.

Thank you.